Cool Yule!

A CREATIVE AND CRAFTY CHRISTMAS

BY DEBRA MOSTOW ZAKARIN
ILLUSTRATED BY DEBRA ZISS

Grosset & Dunlap • New York

ISBN 0-448-43249-8   A B C D E F G H I J

The materials and objects needed for the crafts in this book can be found at your local supermarket, crafts, or hardware store.

Many of the crafts call for the use of a hot-glue gun. This great and essential craft tool can be found for under $10 at your local craft store. Like any craft tool or kitchen utensil—please make sure to be super careful and get a grown-up to supervise. If you don't feel comfortable using a hot-glue gun then substitute with Tacky Glue.

For Patricia, Charlie and Nicholette Kenny—who have not only taught me the true meaning of Christmas, but true friendship—DMZ

In loving memory of Roberta Ziss—DZ

A heartfelt thank you to my editor, Emily Fischer, for her support and insightful comments. And a special thank you to Sandra Gutierrez for her "crafty" assistance.

MERRY CHRISTMAS

Christmas is a time of wonder. It's about trying to figure out why people *still* give out those awful-tasting brick-like fruitcakes year after year. Really! They make great doorstops, but do you know anybody who actually eats those things? *Ugh!*

Seriously though, Christmas is a very special time of the year. It's about spending time with family and friends. It's about reflecting upon your year and gearing up for the new one. It's also about giving gifts. Now, we all know how easy it is to get caught up in the shopping frenzy, but try to let this time of year be the time to truly enjoy what you have, consider what others don't have, and make a difference in someone else's life.

Don't let Christmas become about how many gifts you have under the tree or how much money you need to spend on someone else. Stop. Look into your heart. Let this year be different. Sure, store-bought gifts are totally awesome, but in the end it's the homemade ones that people treasure most. In this book, you'll learn how to make this Christmas totally cool with lots of groovy crafts, recipes, and games.

However you celebrate this beautiful holiday, remember the true meaning of Christmas is about being with family and friends, helping others who aren't able to help themselves, and being tolerant and loving to others—no matter what their belief and faith is. Change begins with someone great—you!

So, what are you waiting for? Gather your friends and family together and have yourself a very Merry Christmas!

COOL YULE PLANNER

How's a groovy gal like you going to get it all done before Christmas? It is way too easy to get stressed a few weeks before the 25th of December. And stress is no good! Panic no more. This *Cool Yule Planner* will make your holiday happy, fun, and hassle-free.

Let the countdown to Christmas begin—three, two, one . . . and you're off...

Third Week of November

❄ Get permission from the folks to throw a Cool Yule Christmas Bash (a.k.a, CYCB.) Now would be a good time to talk money (a.k.a, party budget.)

❄ Make a party invite list.

❄ Make a *"Gift For"* list of all family and friends you plan on giving gifts to (next to their names write down ideas of what you plan on giving them – like a cool craft made exclusively by you.)

❄ Sending out Christmas cards? Make a list of all family and friends you will be sending them to (give yourself a break and send cards to only those friends and relatives who live out-of-town.)

Last Week of November

❄ Sort through all of your craft materials (i.e. buttons, ribbons, lace, glue, paper, and so on) and see what you have and what you need.

❄ Take advantage of Thanksgiving sales and buy all the materials you will need to make the hippest gifts (use the *"Gift For"* list as a reference so that you don't forget anyone.)

❄ Make invites for your CYCB (don't forget, the more the merrier.)

First Week of December

❄ Plan CYCB menu

❄ Make your Christmas cards, wreaths, and ornaments

❄ Mail CYCB invitations

Second Week of December

❄ Make gifts for friends and family

❄ Send out Christmas cards

❄ Hang Christmas lights

❄ Hang wreaths

❄ As the Christmas cards come in, display them around the house or your room

Third Week of December

❄ Wrap Christmas gifts

❄ Shop for CYCB food

* Make gingerbread house

* Choose Christmas tree and decorate with family

* Hang Christmas stockings

* Simmer cinnamon sticks so your home smells sweet like Christmas

* Hang mistletoe (symbol of peace and love)

The Days Before Christmas

* Make Christmas cookies

* Prepare any food for your CYCB that can be made a few days beforehand

* Make sure you have some small last minute gifts on hand for that "unexpected" visitor

Pat yourself on the back for a job well done—you did it! Now you can have a blast at your Cool Yule Christmas Bash. Merry Christmas!

FA-LA-LA FACTS!

❋ The Christmas wreath displayed on the front door is a symbol of welcome and long life to all who enter.

❋ For every Christmas tree harvested, two to three seedlings are planted in its place.

❋ Due to all the time zones in the world, Santa has 31 hours to deliver gifts. This means he has to visit 832 homes every second. *(How does he do it?!)*

❋ The first postage stamp to commemorate Christmas was issued in 1937 in Austria.

❋ In 1836, Alabama was the first state in the United States to declare Christmas a legal holiday.

❋ Christmas trees are grown in all 50 states, including Hawaii and Alaska.

❋ Most artificial trees are manufactured in Korea, Taiwan, or Hong Kong.

❋ Poinsettias are the most popular Christmas plant and are the number-one flowering potted plant in the United States.

❄ Bing Crosby's song, *White Christmas*, is the best-selling Christmas single of all time.

❄ January 6th is the traditional end of the Christmas holiday, and the date decorations and trees are taken down. According to folklore, to do so earlier will bring bad luck for the rest of the year.

❄ In 1822, the Postmaster of Washington D.C. complained that he had to add 16 mailmen during the holiday to deal with Christmas cards alone. He wanted to limit the number of cards a person could send. He wrote, "I don't know what we'll do if this keeps on."

❄ The first commercial Christmas cards (1,000 total) were designed in 1843 by J.C. Horsley and were sold in London, England.

❄ Thomas Edison invented the electric light bulb in 1879. Three years later, Edward H. Johnson, an employee at Edison's company had Christmas-tree bulbs specially made. However, they weren't mass produced until a few years later.

❄ People didn't begin exchanging Christmas gifts until the late 1800's.

COOL AND CRAFTY  CHRISTMAS GIFTS

RAD MAGAZINE RACK

Do you have a gal pal, cousin, Aunt who just can't get her hands on enough magazines? How about making a personalized magazine rack just for her? This rad reading rack makes a great and useful Christmas gift for all avid readers.

Here's what you need:

Three empty cereal boxes

Tacky glue

Magazines

Scissors

Decorative stuff (i.e. lace, ribbons, rhinestones)

Here's what you do:

❄ Take three empty cereal boxes and cut away the flaps at the top of the box.

❄ Cut away the top third of one of the side panels on each of the boxes.

❄ Round off the corners.

❄ Align the boxes and glue them together side by side.

❄ Using old magazines, make a collage around the outside of the boxes.

You can even jazz it up by gluing on some rhinestones and funky ribbons. *If you have some funds left over, give a magazine subscription along with this rad magazine rack.*

This gift is also perfect for your brother or guy friend who collects comic books. Instead of making a collage of old magazines, use old comic books.

CHRISTMAS TO A T-PILLOW

These **T-** pillows really allow your creativity to run wild! Great for gifts or to add ambience to your party room. Go wild!

Here's what you need:

Clean white T-shirt (the size of the T-shirt will determine the size of the pillow)

Polyester or cotton stuffing

Cardboard

Needle and thread (or sewing machine)

Fabric paint

Here's what you do:

❄ Place a piece of cardboard between the front and back of the T-shirt and decorate with fabric paint (the cardboard will prevent the paint from leaking through.)

❄ Design any way you like. It can be a Christmas theme or just something decorative. Let dry completely.

❄ Sew the armholes and bottom of the T-shirt closed. Don't sew up the head opening yet.

❄ Stuff it. Push the polyester or cotton stuffing in through the head opening—don't forget about getting it into the sleeves.

❄ Sew the hole for the head closed.

❄ Buy lots of T-shirts because you won't be able to stop at just one pillow. They are that cute!

<u>Sewing tip</u>: Turn the T-shirt inside out and then sew up the holes. This way you won't be able to see the stitches when you turn the T-shirt the right side out.

15

NIFTY NECKLACES

Set an evening aside when you and your sibs or even some pals sit down at the kitchen table and make these nifty necklaces for friends and family. Imagine you are famous jewelry designers...and let your creativity flow!

Here's what you need:

Self-hardening clay or oven-bake clay (if using oven-bake, make sure to have a grown-up supervise)

Candy or soap molds—can be found at any craft store (these molds come in various shapes: sea shells, stars, hearts, Christmas shapes, etc.)

Toothpick

Acrylic paints

Acrylic spray

Nylon thread

Necklace clasps

Beads

Here's what you do:

❄ Put pieces of clay into the candy molds (or shape them free-form however you like.)

❄ Use the toothpick to poke a hole through the shapes once they have hardened a bit.

❄ Let clay pieces dry completely—this will take about a couple of days and you will know when they are dry because they will be hard to the touch. Or, if using oven-bake clay, bake pieces according to directions.

❄ If you used one, remove pieces from mold.

❄ Paint the dry shapes any way you like. Let dry.

❄ Spray on a coat of acrylic. Let dry.

❄ String the clay pieces and beads onto the nylon thread and attach the clasp.

GORGEOUS
Simply gorgeous!

STOCKING TOPPERS

A cute change from attaching a gift card on top of a gift is a stocking topper. These small and easy-to-make felt stockings will give your gift that extra homemade holiday touch.

Here's what you need:

Felt
Fabric paint
Needle and thread
Rhinestones

Glue gun
Hole puncher
Scissors

Here's what you do:

❄ Cut your felt (any color you choose) into the shape of a Christmas stocking. Remember, this is going on top of a present so don't make it too big.

❄ Sew together the sides of the pieces of felt, leaving the top open.

❄ Now, decorate by gluing on rhinestones or by writing the recipient's name with fabric paint.

❄ Punch a hole through the top so you can attach the topper to a ribbon on the gift.

❄ "Stuff" the stocking topper with a piece of chocolate or candy.

❄ Remember, presentation is everything!

BEADED CANDY CANES

This easy and fun way to make craft can be used for so many things: as a gift wrapping "top" topper, a CYCB prize, or even as a toe-riffic sandal accessory.
The possibilities are endless.

Here's what you need:

Pipe cleaners (one for each topper)

Red and white beads

Here's what you do:

❋ Knot one end of the pipe cleaner.

❋ Thread the beads through the pipe in any color design you choose. You can use alphabet beads to write the gift recipient's name on the pipe cleaner for that much-appreciated personal touch.

❋ Knot the other end of the pipe cleaner.

❋ Bend the top portion to look like the curve of a candy cane.

SIMPLY TOE-RIFFIC SANDALS

This is one sandal you're sure to flip over. Your friend's feet will be all-the-rage this season. Even though it's winter time, this toe-riffic sandal can be used for the shower, at the gym, or as a gift for that friend who is going to some warm tropical island over the Christmas break. You may want to consider making one for yourself, so as not to have fancy-feet envy.

Here's what you need:

Plain flip-flop sandals (these inexpensive sandals can be found at most drugstores.)

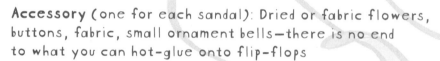

Hot-glue gun

Accessory (one for each sandal): Dried or fabric flowers, buttons, fabric, small ornament bells—there is no end to what you can hot-glue onto flip-flops

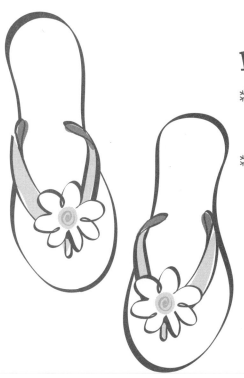

Here's what you do:

❄ Hot-glue the accessory of your choice to the flip-flops.

❄ Got a friend who just loves daisies—glue them! Yup, that's it. Simple to do—however, the challenge is thinking of your recipient. To make this gift something really special, wrap it up with some nail polish and toe separators for a pampered gal pal who just can't live without her monthly pedicure.

If sandals aren't your thing, grab your hot-glue gun and jazz up a plain wool hat, scarf, or gloves with some cute accessories—like pom-poms, ornamental bells, or anything else to get rid of the holiday chill and bring in some fashionable holiday cheer.

KEEP IN TOUCH

With this awesome stationery box as a gift, that friend from sleep-away camp, brother or sister at college, or cousin who lives far away has absolutely, positively *no* excuse for NOT keeping in touch.

Here's what you need:

Unfinished wood box—the size of a shoebox or even a bit smaller. Look around your house, garage sales, or at your local craft store. If you can't find one, or you are working within a *really* tight budget, you can even use a shoebox.

Pencil

Acrylic paints

Acrylic spray

Scissors

Photo of you or one with you and the recipient of the gift

Contact paper

Crafts glue

Glitter glue

Here's what you do:

❇ Draw a design on all sides of the box with your pencil. Be creative. Draw something that truly captures the relationship you share with the person receiving this great gift. For example, if both of you love the movies or going to the theatre, draw film reels and popcorn. You can also make a design or collage using magazine or playbill cut outs, ticket stubs, and empty candy wrappers. Leave some space for the photo.

❇ If you painted the design, let it dry.

❇ Once the paint dries completely, spray with acrylic. Let dry.

❇ Next, glue the photo on the box. Outline it with glitter glue, ribbon, lace, buttons, or rhinestones.

❇ You can line the inside of the box with contact paper or leave it plain.

❇ Finally, fill the box with either homemade or store-bought stationery. (To really get your point across, pre-address the envelopes to you!)

CUDDLE-UP CUP O' COCOA

Hot cocoa is the perfect drink after an intense snowball fight or to sip while admiring all of your holiday decorations. It also makes a perfect gift for that special someone. Present this cocoa mix in a glass jar and tie ribbon around it. Don't forget to stick a label on it with the instructions.

Here's what you need:

10 1/2 cups nonfat dry milk powder   Glass jar

6 ounces nondairy creamer   Ribbon

1 pound quick chocolate milk mix   White adhesive label

1/3 cup sugar

Here's what you do:

❆ In a large bowl, combine all of the ingredients. Stir together well.

❆ Pour mix into glass jars and tie decorative ribbons around the lids.

❆ On white adhesive labels write the following directions:

Combine 1/4 cup cocoa mix and 3/4 cup boiling water into a cup.
Stir well and mmmmm, enjoy!

LET IT SPARKLE, LET IT SPARKLE

The next craft makes a great pin or picture frame. So flash those pearly whites and bring on the Christmas sparkle.

Here's what you need:

Crafts glue
Photo of YOU
Poster board (just a little bigger than your photo— 1/2 inch or so)
Ruler
Scissors

Sparkly beads (assorted colors), sequins or fabric
Jewelry-pin backing (if making a pin)
Frame hanger or stand (these stands are a great and inexpensive way to display a photo)

Here's what you do:

❄ Glue the photo to the poster board.

❄ Cut the poster board so that there is at least a 1/4-inch border around the photo.

❄ Glue sparkly beads, sequins, or fabric around the photo.

❄ If you're making a pin, glue the jewelry-pin backing to the back.

❄ If making a frame, glue the frame-hanger on the back or place in a photo stand.

❄ If making this as a pin, smaller photos work best. And, oh, Grandmas really dig this gift.

RRRRRRING HOLDER

This ring holder will make the supreme gift for your mom, your gal pal who has a thing for rings, or even your favorite manicurist. And while you're at it, since you've got two hands, make one for yourself.

Here's what you need:

Cardboard

Scissors

Felt in three different colors

Two craft sticks (you can get these at your craft store; they are similar to popsicle sticks, but heavier)

Styrofoam

Round metal lid from a jar

Glue

Two 8-inch pieces of ribbon

Clothespin or chip-clip (something that can be used as a "clamp")

Here's what you do:

❋ Place your hand flat on a piece of cardboard with your fingers spread apart and, carefully, trace.

❋ Cut out your traced hand.

❋ Using the cardboard cut out as the pattern; trace the hand onto two different pieces of felt (of the same color.) Carefully, cut each of them.

✷ Glue craft sticks to the bottom of both sides of the cardboard hand. Align the sticks so that one is on top of the other.

✷ Spread glue on one side of the cardboard and place one felt hand on top of the glue. Repeat on the other side with the other piece of felt.

✷ With the second piece of felt cut two small pieces—this will be the bottom of the sleeve. Glue the sleeves on each side of the hand and clamp down with a clothespin or chip-clip, until dry.

✷ With the third colored piece of felt cut out oval or square shapes and glue them on as fingernails. They will look like "polished" nails.

✷ Cut a piece of Styrofoam to fit inside of the metal lid and glue it there.

✷ Glue some felt around the metal lid and plastic foam.

✷ Use the scissors to poke a small hole in the felt-covered plastic foam. The foam, which is sturdy, will steady the hand and enable it to stand upright.

✷ Put some glue in the hole and on the end of a crafts stick, which is attached to the hand, and place it in the hole.

✷ Decorate the stick with either ribbon, glitter glue, or nail stickers.

FRIENDS 4-EVER FRIENDSHIP RING

If you plan on giving this to your best girlfriend why not make her a *Christmassy* friendship ring and place it on her new ring holder?

Friendship rings are the kind of thing you'll keep for years to come in your special keepsake box.

Here's what you need:

Wire, string, or a pipe cleaner

Beads (use green and red to show your Christmas spirit)

Here's what you do:

❄ With the wire, string, or pipe cleaner, measure your ring finger and leave a bit of extra slack to tie the ends together.

❄ Create a cool pattern.

❄ Bead away.

Place your friendship ring on the Rrrrrrring Holder and your gal pal has got an awesome Christmas gift. Make an extra one for yourself.

BRING ON THE SNOW

No matter where you live, Christmas just isn't Christmas without some snow. So, even if you live in the desert, bring on the storm! These snow globes make super-cute table decorations as well as great gifts for little kids.

Here's what you need:

Clean baby-food or pickle jars (or any glass jar with a lid)
Florist clay
Small figurine (like a snowman, Santa Claus, seashells—anything that is small and waterproof)
Fake snow or white glitter
Hot-glue gun
Plastic greenery
Ribbon

Here's what you do:

❄ Glue some florist clay to the inside of the jar's lid.

❄ Attach the greenery to the florist clay with glue.

❄ Using cold water, fill the jar to about 1/2 inch from the top.

❄ Sprinkle 2 tablespoons (more for a larger jar) of white glitter or fake snow into the jar.

❄ Drop in the figurine.

❄ Seal with the lid (the base of the snow globe) and wrap a ribbon around the lid.

SENTIMENTAL STICKS

Good thing you didn't throw out the old Christmas cards that were strung across your wall last year. With some scissors and cinnamon sticks you've got a sweet gift for your aunt, uncle, favorite teacher, or to a person of your choosing.

Here's what you need:

Recycled Christmas card with sayings such as: "Peace on Earth," "Joy to the World," "Wishing you Joy, Peace and Happiness."

Scissors

Pencil

Ruler

Red pen

Red and green paper

Glue stick

Cinnamon sticks

Hot-glue gun

Gold string

Green or red ribbon

Here's what you do:

❄ Take your Christmas card and draw a box around the saying, leaving a 1/2 inch border.

❄ Cut the phrase out and outline it in red marker.

❄ Cut a piece of green paper about 1/4 inch larger than the saying.

❄ Cut a piece of red paper 1 inch larger than the green paper.

❄ With the glue stick, glue the green paper onto the red paper.

❄ Then, glue the saying onto the green paper.

❄ Hot-glue eight cinnamon sticks along the border of the paper: two sticks on the top, two sticks on the bottom, and two sticks on each side (the sticks should be larger than the paper.)

❄ Tie the gold cord for hanging from the top corners.

❄ Tie each of the intersecting corners with the ribbon.

'TIS THE SEASON TO PAMPER

Do you know somebody who does everything for everybody else, but never takes time for themselves? Nope, not talking about you, sister. I'm talking about that *somebody else*. With that in mind, put together some Pamper Thyself baskets for that important person who doesn't take the time to pamper herself. Fill them up with nail polish, nail files, washcloths, and a bunch of other cool pampering stuff you can make on your own (you may even want to include a pair of Simply Toe-riffic Sandals.)

SIMPLE SOAP

Here's what you need:

Glycerin soap in lots of different colors

Soap or candy molds—in hip and different shapes (craft stores sell these)

Olive oil spray (sold at all supermarkets)

Microwave

Microwavable cups

Oven gloves or potholders

Wooden popsicle sticks

Sharp knife

Here's what you do:

❄ Cut each bar of soap into three pieces.

❄ Put a piece into each microwavable cup (or experiment by mixing several different colors of soap.)

❄ Place the cup in the microwave on high for about 15 seconds to melt the soap.

❄ With oven gloves or potholders remove cup from the microwave and stir with a wooden Popsicle stick. (CAREFUL: melted soap will be very hot!)

❄ Working quickly (you don't want the soap to harden just yet,) pour the mixture into molds which have been pre-sprayed with olive oil (this will keep the soon-to-be-hardened soap from sticking to the mold.)

❄ After 10 minutes the soap will be hard and cool. Now you can remove it from the mold and put in a bath bag.

(KEEP ON GOING . . .)

BUBBLING BATH BAGS

Here's what you need:

Washcloths

Ribbon

Thread

Sewing needle

Scissors

Sewing machine (if you know how to use one)

Here's what you do:

❄ Fold a washcloth in half.

❄ Fold a ribbon in half lengthwise and place it, folded edges in, inside the open top of the washcloth.

❄ Sew up each side (including the side where the ribbon is.)

❄ Turn the washcloth inside out and fill with Simple Soap or Bathing Beauty Bath Salts.

❄ Tie the bag closed with the ribbon.

BATHING BEAUTY BATH SALTS

Here's what you need:

Large mixing bowl

Two cups Epsom salts

One cup sea salt, rock salt or coarse salt

Food coloring

1/4 teaspoon glycerin

Essential oil for fragrance
(vanilla, peppermint, peach, rose...)

Dry jars with metal screw-on lids
(clean baby-food jars are perfect)

Here's what you do:

❄ In a bowl, combine all salts and mix.

❄ Add a couple of drops of food coloring.

❄ Add the glycerin and mix.

❄ Add about 5 drops of essential oil and mix well.

❄ Spoon salt into the jars and close them.

Make up a gift tag that says something like, "Use about 1/2 cup in the bath and have yourself a very merry Christmas." Or fill the Bubbling Bath Bags up with some Bathing Beauty Bath Salts.

CORK IT!

Are you always looking for a place to post all of your notes, pictures, party invites, and autographs? Well, so are your friends! That's why you are number-one friend and gift giver. Think about who this bulletin board is for and plan your design accordingly.

Here's what you need:

Cork sheet—about 11" x 17"

Fabric (3 1/2 inches larger than the finished design piece; you want this much extra fabric so you can stretch it tightly behind the cork board)

Spray-adhesive glue and white-bottled glue

Staples

Exacto knife (ask a grown-up to help you with this)

Scissors

Ribbon

Here's what you do:

❄ Draw your design on the cork sheet, for example, the number "1" (get it? as in number-one friend)

❄ Carefully cut out the shape with the knife (make sure a grown-up is there to assist.)

❄ Spray the board with adhesive glue and place glue-side down on the underside (the wrong side) of the fabric.

❄ Neatly and patiently, pull back the fabric and flatten the edges—basically, you are covering the corkboard with the fabric.

❄ Glue and staple down the excess fabric (you can cut some if necessary to make it as smooth as possible.) Pull *very tight* to avoid wrinkles.

❄ If you like, glue ribbon along the edges for the trim.

To Do:
Find some funky thumbtacks, and someone's got a great gift.

MOD MONITOR

Wanna know who spends too much time in front of the computer? That would be EVERYBODY! Wanna know who stares at a dull-looking computer? Everybody! No more, though, now that you're giving away Mod Monitor computer frames.

Here's what you need:

Two foam sheets for the frame (they come in different colors and can be found at any craft store.)

Glue

Scissors

Self-adhesive Velcro

Ruler

Glitter paint or craft paint

Here's what you do:

❄ Measure and write down the dimensions of the monitor screen. Do this from the flat outer "trim" of the monitor (the part that faces you) just to the inside of where the screen begins.

✳ Following the measurements, cut a frame out of the foam sheet.

✳ Use the leftover foam to make designs to glue on the monitor frame. Your design can be abstract or have a theme like: mini pictures of you and the recipient, snow scenes, beach scenes, moon and stars, or anything else you choose.

✳ Cut about 1-inch long strips of Velcro and attach it to the back of each side of the monitor.

Since you're in computer mode—why not design a cute mouse pad? Cut a cool shape (a mouse pad doesn't have to be the usual square or round shape) out of the craft foam sheet. Merry Christmas and have fun surfing the internet!

HIP HAIR CLIPS

These hip hair-clips can make great stocking stuffers as well as groovy game prizes.

Here's what you need:

Plain, metal hair-clips (the kind that snap back and forth, also known as claw clips)

Colored and glittered nail polish (*total secret*: nail polish works great as "paint" for barrettes—not only are there fun and great colors to choose from, but it rarely chips!)

Acrylic spray

Tiny rhinestone beads

Super glue

Here's what you do:

❄ Paint the hair clips with colored or glitter nail polish. Let dry.

❄ Spray with acrylic spray. Let dry.

❄ Glue on rhinestone beads. Let glue dry. If you like, try using some puffy paint.

❄ Spray again with acrylic spray.

IT'S A DOG'S LIFE

Your little Fifi already has a dog's life, so make it official with her very own tree ornament. Remember, 'tis the season so spread Christmas cheer around. Bow-wow.

Here's what you need:

White craft-foam

Pen

Dog bone-shaped stencil or cookie-cutter
(if you can't find a stencil or cookie-cutter
in this shape you can always draw it free hand)

Scissors

Hole punch

Green and red paint

Green and red ribbon

Here's what you do:

❄ Trace the bone onto the frame and cut it out.

❄ At the top of each end of the bone, punch a hole (so you have two holes.)

❄ Paint the bone green or red. Let dry.

❄ Write your pup's name in green or red (the opposite color of the bone.) Let dry.

❄ Thread some ribbon through the holes, and you've got yourself a beautiful, barkin' bone ornament.

GROOVY GARLANDS

Garlands are so much fun to make, especially with a bunch of friends. Sit around the table, chat away about what you plan on doing over Christmas break and go, go groovy garlands!

Here's what you need:

Waxed dental floss or string

Scissors

Needle

Colored popcorn (can be found during the holiday season at the supermarket)

Beads

Jelly beans

Cranberries

Rhinestone beads

Buttons

Here's what you do:

❄ Cut a piece of dental floss, string, or fishing wire to the length you'd like your garland to be.

❄ Thread a needle with floss or string.

❄ Push the needle through whatever object you are stringing.

❄ String on the objects in a pattern, or haphazardly. You can even mix objects to make the garland super groovy. When finished, knot the end to secure. Hang the garland on the Christmas tree, over your fireplace, on a door, or by your staircase.

SWEET AS SUGAR WREATH

Okay, so you're not quite sure how to let your cute science-lab partner know that you like him? No need. Just smile and give him a Sweet as Sugar Wreath. If that isn't hint enough, girl, he's just not smart enough for you!

Here's what you need:

Styrofoam wreath—standard size (can be found at your local crafts store)

Ribbon (one with a pattern will work well)

Hot-glue gun

Hard candy in various shapes, sizes and colors

Here's what you do:

❄ Wrap the wreath tightly with ribbon (wind the ribbon around the wreath, overlapping it just a bit so it hides the Styrofoam) and secure with glue.

❄ Arrange the candy on the wreath.

❄ One by one, glue each piece of candy to the wreath.

❄ Loop the left over ribbon through the wreath and tie a knot.

Hang this wreath in the kitchen or give it to a friend with a sweet tooth. This also makes a great gift for your sweetheart or favorite teacher.

TAKE COVER

This marbleized lampshade makes a great gift for your mom's or pop's office or for that person who loves to read in bed at night.

Here's what you need:

Metal pan (the disposable kind)

Liquid starch

Acrylic paints

Skewer (or any kind of thin wooden stick)

Small lampshade—you can use either cloth or paper

Waxed paper (or cloth)

Here's what you do:

❄ Pour liquid starch into a metal pan, about 1-inch deep.

❄ Drip whatever paint colors you choose into the starch—using no more than two colors at a time (if you use more than two colors, it will not create a swirl/marbleized effect.)

❄ If the paint is too thick, thin it out with a bit of water.

❄ Use the skewer to swirl the paint into the starch. Be careful not to mix them too much.

❄ Gently, roll the lampshade over the surface of the liquid. This will give the lampshade a cool marbleized look.

❄ Remove the lampshade and let it dry on wax paper.

❄ After it has dried, you can hand-paint some special touches like flowers, a Christmas tree, or even the Eiffel Tower.

Think about the interests of the recipient and go wild. If you have some money left over, buy a base to go along with the lampshade.

GODDESS COOKBOOK

Are you known for your cooking or baking skills? Now you can share your secret recipes with your loved ones by making your very own cookbook!

Here's what you need:

5 x 7- inch index cards (use one card per recipe and about 8–10 recipes per book)

Colored markers and crayons

Black fine-point marker

Hole-punch

Decorative ribbon or binder ring

Here's what you do:

❄ If you're known for a culinary specialty, make that your recipe book, for example, "Pizza Pizzazz," "Incredible Edible Cookies," or "Simply Soups".

❄ On each index card neatly hand-write a recipe with the black fine-point marker.

※ Decorate the borders with the colored markers and crayons. You can try your hand at drawing the finished product, or include photographs.

※ Don't forget to make a cover for your book, which will include the title and author (that's you!). You may also want to add a card before the recipes for a dedication, "For Grandma...the real cooking Goddess".

※ Next, at the top left corner of the cards punch a hole and string a decorative ribbon through or use a binder ring.

※ If your budget allows, laminate each card BEFORE running a ribbon through.

Carrie's Xmas Cookies

PERSONALIZED STOCKING STUFFERS

According to Christmas folklore, the first gifts ever given by Santa were to three poor girls (they had left their only pairs of socks hanging by the fire) who needed money for their weddings. And, wouldn't you know it, Santa left each of them gold coins in their stockings. To carry on this tradition, we hang stockings over our fireplaces, across a wall, along the staircase banister or even over a window, making it easy for Santa, or anyone else, to drop a few extra trinkets our way. Here's a fun spin on an old tradition: personalized stocking stuffers! Create a stocking with a specific theme. All you need are socks, a few small gifts and a lot of imagination.

For example, if your dad's an avid golfer, fill up golf socks with golf balls, putting tees, a golf book, and some sunscreen. Is your sister a dancer? Fill a pair of pink tights with a leotard, hair scrunchies, a *Nutcracker* CD, and a bottle of peppermint foot cream.

Santa better watch out! Looks like he's got some competition!

DOIN' SOMETHIN' DIFFERENT

Here are some ideas to put you in the Christmas spirit:

❄ Put on your own Christmas show and videotape it. You can watch it year after year.

❄ Put together a basket of homemade baked goods and hand-deliver it to the local retirement or nursing home.

❄ Give your mail carrier a thermos of hot chocolate.

❄ Collect the books that you don't want and donate them to a school in need.

❄ Play some board games and listen to Christmas music.

❄ Go sledding.

❄ Sit with your family and look through picture albums of past holidays.

❄ Put photos of Christmases past into albums with your family.

❄ Shovel a neighbor's driveway—for free.

❄ Gather together all the gifts you received that you won't use; take them to your local shelter.

❄ With your family, decide on a cause to "adopt" in the coming year. Discuss what you will do as a family to make a difference. Instead of buying each other gifts, make a donation to that charity in someone's honor.

CHRISTMAS MERRIMENT

There are many different traditions of how and when to sit down for Christmas dinner. Some families join together Christmas Eve, others gather on Christmas day.

Do something special this year at your Christmas bash—a buffet with finger foods! Set out small paper plates and napkins with cute Christmas designs. Make the buffet even more festive looking and scatter green and red jelly beans around the table.

SPINACH DIP

"Yuck," you may say to spinach, but this tasty, creamy dip might just change your mind.

Here's what you need:

Six ounces frozen spinach, defrosted

1/2 cup sour cream

Two tablespoons mayonnaise

Pinch of salt

Pinch of black pepper

Here's what you do:

❄ Drain the spinach in a strainer.

❄ Pat dry with paper towel.

❄ Mix together all of the ingredients until smooth.

> Serve the dip in a small bowl and surround it with different colored vegetables—it will look like a veggie wreath.

SIMPLY DELICIOUS DANCER AND DASHER

Cute as they may be, these open-face reindeer sandwiches are too tasty not to nibble on.

Here's what you need for *two* sandwiches:

Slice of bread
Peanut butter
Four mini pretzels
Four raisins
Two mini marshmallows

Here's what you do:

❄ Spread the bread with peanut butter and cut it in half, making two equal triangles.

❄ Place one of the triangles in front of you (point facing down.)

❄ Place one mini pretzel (broken in half) on each of the upper corners. These are the antlers.

❄ Place two raisins in the center of the triangle for the eyes.

❄ Place one mini marshmallow at the bottom point for the nose (when making Rudolph, use a maraschino cherry instead of a marshmallow.)

Arrange on a platter.

51

ORNAMENTAL CHEESE BALL

These cheese balls are delicious and really do look like tree ornaments. Make a few and serve them with crackers or lightly toasted pita bread.

Here's what you need (per ornamental ball):

One cup shredded cheddar cheese
Three tablespoons mayonnaise
One packet ranch dressing dip mix
One 8 ounce block of cream cheese
1/2 cup chopped walnuts

Here's what you do:

❅ Except for the walnuts, place all of the ingredients into a bowl and mix together with a spoon.

❅ Wash your hands thoroughly.

❅ Form the mixture into a ball with your hands.

❅ Roll the ball in the nuts.

❅ Wrap in plastic and refrigerate for 24 hours.

Serve with crackers or pita bread.

YULETIDE DOGS

These wieners are so good, you'll want to make them on any occasion.

Here's what you need (this recipe serves about eight):

One 16-ounce package little sausages or mini hotdogs

One 8-ounce jar cocktail sauce

One 8-ounce jar grape jelly

Spicy brown mustard

Here's what you do:

❉ Over low heat, combine the cocktail sauce and grape jelly in a saucepan.

❉ Mix in the little sausages.

❉ Cook until the sausages are hot (about five minutes.)

❉ Place on a large platter.

❉ Dip in spicy mustard. The taste of sweet and spicy together is simply explosive.

LIP-SMACKING GOOD GINGERBREAD HOUSE

What is it about gingerbread houses that make you feel all warm and wintery inside? I don't know, but I do know that a Christmas table just seems empty without one.

Here's what you need:

Six graham crackers

1/4 cup butter

Four cups sifted powdered sugar

Two unbeaten egg whites

One teaspoon vanilla

1/4 teaspoon cream of tartar

Two tablespoons light cream

Pastry tube

Food coloring (optional)

Candy pieces

Here's what you do:

❋ Mix the butter and powdered sugar together with either a fork or a food processor using the pastry blade. You want it to be the consistency of smooth oatmeal.

❋ Add the vanilla, cream of tartar and egg whites and beat well.

❋ Stir in the cream to make the frosting stiff.

❋ Spoon the frosting into a pastry bag (if you want it to be a certain color other than white, mix in a few drops of food coloring before transferring it to the pastry bag.)

❋ Using the frosting as cement, press your graham crackers together in the shape of a house. Use one cracker for the base of the house, one for each side, one for the back, and two for the roof. Ask someone to help you hold the crackers together as you attach them to each other with the frosting.

❋ Decorate the house with small candies (colored candies, chocolates, chocolate kisses, gum drops, or anything you like), using the frosting as glue

CHOCOLATE SPOONS

A delightfully delicious gift for coffee drinkers and chocolate lovers. You'll need to make a lot of these because you won't be able to stop yourself from licking the spoon!

Here's what you need:

Heavy plastic spoons—red or green

Milk chocolate

White chocolate

Chocolate sprinkles

Colored sugar—red and green

Wax paper

Here's what you do:

❋ On the stovetop, in a double boiler, or in the microwave using a microwave-safe bowl, melt the milk chocolate.

❋ Dip the spoons into the chocolate and place them on the wax paper. Let the chocolate set.

❋ Melt the white chocolate.

❋ Dip the milk-chocolate spoon halfway into the white chocolate and place it on the wax paper.

❋ Before the white chocolate sets, sprinkle on some chocolate sprinkles and colored sugar.

If you plan on giving these spoons as gifts, wrap them in clear cellophane and tie them with ribbons. You can even attach a note that says, "Sweet Stirring."

SUGARY SWEET SNOWMEN

These snowmen make great table decorations and are great to munch on, too.

Here's what you need (for each snowman):

Three large marshmallows

White frosting (store-bought or homemade— see recipe from gingerbread house)

Gumdrops

Licorice stick (cut in half)

Small chocolate candies

Here's what you do:

❄ Stack three marshmallows on top of one another using the frosting as glue.

❄ Stick half a piece of licorice into each side of the middle marshmallow (these will be the arms.)

❄ Glue the gumdrop onto the center of the top marshmallow (the snowman's hat.)

❄ Next, glue on the chocolate candies as the buttons.

COOL CHRISTMAS GAMES

DECK THE HALLS

Here's what you need:

Two decks of playing cards

Six to eight (depending upon how many people are playing) small, unwrapped gifts (wrapped candy, lip gloss, or even a bookmark)

Here's what you do:

❋ Shuffle each deck.

❋ Distribute one deck as evenly as possible among the players. You, the dealer, hold on to the second deck of cards.

❋ Flip one card over.

❋ Now, one by one, call out the card in your hand.

✳ The person who has that particular card selects one prize from the table.

✳ Other players must pay close attention to who takes which prize. Once the person has made her choice, she should hide the prize from the other players.

✳ Continue calling out cards until all of the prizes are distributed.

✳ Keep calling off the cards and the person who has the next card must try to remember who has what prize (since there are no more prizes on the table.) So, if Maci wants the lip gloss and she remembers that Jenna has it, she must say, "Jenna, I'll take the lip gloss." Then, Jenna must give her lip gloss to Maci. However, Jenna could win it back later if she remembers who has it.

✳ If a player misses, by incorrectly matching a prize to a player, she forfeits that turn.

✳ Play until all the cards have been called. Whoever ends up with a prize or prizes gets to keep them.

PASS THAT GIFT

Here's what you do:

❄ Wrap a small gift in a small box. Write a message and tape it to the wrapped gift.

❄ Put the box in a slightly larger box, wrap it. Attach a message.

❄ Put that box in a slightly larger box and wrap it. Attach a message. And so on. The more boxes you use, the more fun the game is.

❄ Each message should give simple instructions as to what to do with the gift. For example, "Pass this gift to the person wearing Christmas earrings," "Pass this gift to the person whose name begins with the letter C," "This box goes to the person wearing a sparkly headband," and so on. The final box will also have a message on it.

✳ The message on the biggest box should read something like this, "This gift goes to the person standing closest to the fireplace." That person gets the gift, opens it and finds the next box with a message that could say something like this: "So sorry! This present goes to the person who is sitting next to you on the right!"

✳ Keep passing and opening until you reach the last box. The message on the last box could say, "Open me," or "Merry Christmas to you!"

✳ Don't want the other players to feel disappointed? Surprise them all with a small token (a Christmas candy, jingle bell or candy cane) of your appreciation for being such great sports!

Some Cool Gift Ideas:
Christmas coupons, lipsticks, key rings, CDs, nail polish, diaries, picture frames, clocks, handheld games... the list goes on.

SING OFF

This is a great way to get into the spirit of Christmas. Divide your group into two or three teams (depending upon how many people there are.) Then, every two to three minutes you, as song master, shout out a different word like white, snow, sled, friendship, and so on. The teams will have three minutes to come up with songs that have that word in the title. Whatever team gets the most songs—and is able to sing them—wins that round. Each word is a round. Play about six rounds. The winning team gets a prize. A great gift would be a homemade Christmas song sheet made by you, a Christmas music CD, or even a harmonica for each player on the winning team.

CHRISTMAS SONG SHEET

Christmas is a great time to indulge the closet performer you've got locked away inside. And just because your folks aren't too keen on letting you out at night to serenade the entire neighborhood (also known as Christmas caroling), doesn't mean your pipes shouldn't be put to good use. Make singing songs part of your Christmas celebration before, during, and after. Throw on some cool Christmas tapes, tune into the radio or just sing loud and strong. Keep a bunch of Christmas song sheets (get them laminated) on hand so your friends and family can join in the Christmas cheer.

UNTIL NEXT YEAR . . .

Here's hoping that this Christmas is not only magical, but also crafty and creative! Don't forget that the best thing about holiday time is that it's family and friends time, too. And, of course, reaching out to others is the greatest gift of all. So, until next year, Merry Christmas to all and to all a Happy New Year!

MERRY CHRISTMAS!